straight from my mind

Bibliografische Information der Deutschen
Nationalbibliothek: Die Deutsche
Nationalbibliothek verzeichnet diese
Publikation in der Deutschen
Nationalbibliografie; detaillierte
bibliografische Daten sind im Internet über
dnb.dnb.de abrufbar.

Herstellung und Verlag: BoD – Books on
Demand, Norderstedt

ISBN: 978-3-753-499-796

All images used, as well as the cover, are by
me, Suzan Uyaniker

Contact via Instagram: @suzanlovesart

explanations

trying to explain my feelings

This is for the ones, struggling to express themselves. For those, thriving to be heard and understood. Remember, you are not alone, you are good enough and you have always been. No matter what else people tried to make believe you.

Contents

introduction

Before you dig deeper into my emotions, I will introduce myself. Also with the hope, that you might be able to get a connection to these poems and a feeling of being understood and less of the feelings that make you feel alone. A few words will be enough.

I am Suzie. An average girl with big dreams others probably cannot imagine. I have always been like that and a professional daydreamer as well. Sometimes those dreams even scared me, but I have heard that the dreams that scare you the most, are the best ones. I have had really dark days as well and a long and hard time understanding and realizing that I am not alone with that. I want to share a part of my journey with you through the following poems. It feels like it took me way too long realizing that i am good enough. And I am worthy of taking up space and so are you.

Remember, you are good enough. You are heard by someone, just not everyone shows. Not everyone feels and expresses their feelings as you do. Some are more intense in their ways, some are very shy. Remember, you are loved.

people i love and loved

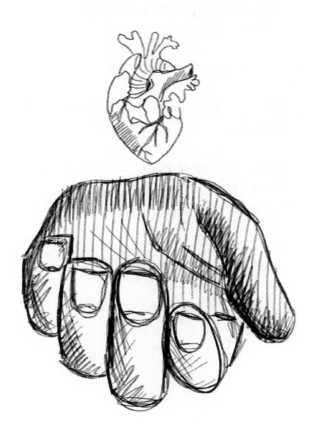

I)

i am a very intense lover

i have always been, there was a time,
when i was even scared of it

    i was afraid to talk

but be sure when i say i love you that
i mean it

because this is something I would
never joke about

II)

when i was in love, i was heavily
scared of showing emotions

that was, because i was so afraid of
getting hurt

    afraid of embarrassing myself

    sometimes, i still am today

because the fear of messing up with
people i love

can be so overwhelming sometimes

III)

once, i was deeply in love with a good
friend of mine

those feelings poked my heart in a
painful way quite often

i never told him, i probably will not do
so in the future too

> i was afraid of making things
> awkward

i struggled between a good friendship
and risking it all to get what i want

> but i was not brave enough to
> take that risk

> i wish i would have been brave
> enough

> i promised myself to do better
> next time

IV)

have you ever been ready to give
your heart to someone who gave his
heart to someone else already?

V)

you used me to fill a void. now that
the void is gone, i am gone for you
too

VI)

i have had days that i would simply
describe as a huge struggle

days, i believed i did not deserve any
of the good in my life

> but there were people who
> never gave up on me

i do not know how i can say thank
you properly

but to my family and my real friends

> i love you so much

VII)

a simple statement: i love my family
and my real friends.

VIII)

accept that people you love
eventually will annoy you sometimes.
as well as the other way around. that
doesn't mean you're not loved by
them. it doesn't mean that you
suddenly don't love them anymore
too, right?

IX)

while giving so much of your love
and energy to others, don't forget to
protect your own energy and love

 don't forget to love yourself

and don't forget to take enough rest,
you can't pour from an empty cup,
right?

X)

self-love is important

on a daily basis

put yourself first.

be your number one.

everything else will fall in place

XI)

people being intimidated by your
confidence will magically disappear,
sometimes in a painful way,
sometimes quietly

don't limit yourself just to fit in

i mean, why would you wear a jeans
that you probably do not fit in
(anymore)? doesn't that hurt your
tummy? look for that jeans that
makes you glow and comfortable

XII)

sometimes also people you love
might hurt or disappoint you

do not hesitate to speak up for
yourself and your feelings

remember, your feelings are valid,
they will understand and even if they
don't

your feelings are still valid

anxiety and fear

I)

it is time to calm down

> but the thoughts in the back of
> my head are creeping on

> > until they overwhelm me

until they take away my ability to
speak and breathe

II)

one breath,

two breath, the third and fourth one
all in one

    Am i even breathing?

    where am i?

    i am not safe, i do not feel safe

    in reality i am safe

    but i do not feel so

    first tear

        second tear

           all tears all at once

until my body meets the floor again

III)

after realizing i met the floor so
often, i realized i needed more help
than i thought, even though i was
still able to manage a lot of things

facing what bothers and triggers me
was hard and full of tears, but also
full of enlightening moments

    also full of joy

and the relieve of realizing my full
potential

and especially realizing that I am
loved

    for who i am

with both the light and the dark

IV)

even though i faced my fears and saw
the first bits of my progress

    i experienced setbacks

    i experienced a few

    it was frustrating

    but to be fair, easier each time

    it gave me new hope

spoiler alert: setbacks are parts of
your healing journey

another spoiler alert: they don't
define you. keep on going, you are
stronger than you think

V)

small events, not even worthy to
think about

    are sometimes the thief of my
    peace

    the thief of my sleep

VI)

i fear some things others probably
wouldn't

but the thing i fear the most is

that everyone i love will eventually
leave me some day

VII)

the fear of failing was often the fear
that kept me from doing great things

      as soon as i let go, i bloomed
      like i never did before

      but the process of letting go can
      be painful

      to face your emotions

to actually feel them instead of
avoiding them

VIII)

one thing that seems to be addictive
and that i need to let go of for sure is
constantly apologizing

sometimes it's not you owing an
apology to someone, but others to
you

pressure and
success

I)

i want to give everything

as always

    i feel the pressure

    i feel like i am not able to move
    my feet

    this invisible wall in front of my
    chest

i need to break it down

i feel stuck

II)

the wall is crumbling

with each crumble falling down i feel
more power to achieve great things

    i feel the pressure on me again

overworking to cope with emotions

        probably not coping,

        but rather ignoring them

III)

my goals

in clear sight

one reached, next one already
planned

one goal after another after
another

i only need to remember myself
to take care of myself too

to take care of my loved ones

constantly need to remember
myself

IV)

i see the first small steps

>towards the person I truly am

>to embrace myself

>to embrace every single step

>no matter how small

>no matter what it is

>as long as it's for my wellbeing

V)

my biggest success probably is to
finally start accepting who i am

to forgive myself

to finally being gentle to myself

VI)

no matter how much stress is going
on, try to not forget about yourself

alone time is important, food is
important, sleep is important, your
social contacts are important and
what ever else is important to you

your inner peace and mental health
definitely are a priority

be your number one

darkest days

I)

people see me as hard working

but my closest ones always see when
i crumble under the pressure that i
created myself

sometimes, it takes so much energy
for simple things

    like eating properly

II)

sometimes when i look into the
mirror

    i see an ugly person

    i talk harshly to myself

i feel terrible for being mad at things
people have done to me that hurt me

    even if they hurt me

    it feels like it is all my fault

III)

sometimes i do not want to accept
the bad days, the bad feelings

    even though i know they have
    their validation as well

IV)

sometimes it feels like i do not
deserve any good

i doubt everything

it just feels like it is too good to be
true

sometimes it is hard for me to trust
anyone

V)

some days, i do not need any
moisturizer for my skincare

> because my tears do a pretty
> good damn job

moisturizing my entire face

> literally, my entire face

VI)

i want to scream

VII)

to anyone that told me, or maybe
also someone that told you, that you
have no reason to be sad

or people that asked you why you are
sad, not with the intention to
understand you, but rather to make
you feel like you're hard to
understand

i have something to say too

shut up. thank you.

and no, (insert a reason that makes
you happy), is not a reason for not
being allowed to ever feel sad again

VIII)

being sad is okay. each of the
emotions you feel are a part of you

you are doing great

i know it is hard to accept your
feelings sometimes

i send you support, in case nobody
else does

IX)

long story short: all of your feelings
are valid. i mean, if a house is
burning, but you don't want it to
burn, does it make it stop burning?
unless you don't have any
superpowers, it won't.

look at that burning house, feel the
fear, think of what a good reaction
might be and try to fight that fire.
depending on the size of the fire, you
might need help. and that's fine.

X)

get some rest tonight

relief and freedom

I)

when i finally had the courage to feel
    my feelings

    to cry my eyes out

    i started to feel relieved

    as if the ocean of tears washed
    away any sorrow for a moment

II)

letting go is painful

    accepting the truth is painful

realizing that people do not love you
as much as you love them is painful

    failing can be painful

there can be so much pain for any
reason that is painful for you

but as soon as you let go, as soon as
you allow yourself to feel

    trust me, it gets better

    yeah, i know, you have probably
    heard that phrase so many
    times

    and no, that doesn't mean your
    feelings are not valid

    but from own experiences

it gets better

just think of all the storms you
have passed

all the dark days that filled up
with light again

try to breathe for a moment

i beg you to not give up

III)

as soon as i accepted myself for who i
am

i experienced a whole another level
of freedom

IV)

the freedom to express yourself,

to allow yourself to communicate
whatever you want

is probably the greatest one

V)

traveling is the most privileged kind
of freedom i was able to experience
so far

VI)

 being who i truly am around my
friends is freedom

VII)

my family accepting me as i am is
freedom

VIII)

but most importantly, allowing
yourself to be you is freedom

happiness

I)

i felt happiness the moment i realized

it starts within me

.

II)

to me, happiness is spending time
        with my loved ones, a time to
        focus on what is really
        important to me

III)

but also success, reaching my goals i
        worked hardly for

IV)

also good food, comfort food is not
        called comfort food for no
        reason

V)

before i forget, also a day full of naps

VI)

painting, being creative is probably
      one of my greatest forms of
      happiness, when words fail
      creativity helps me out

VII)

sharing my happiness with others
      also makes me happy

VIII)

traveling makes me happy and
      excited

IX)

learning new things

X)

it is probably an endless list

XI)

what makes you truly happy?

acknowledgements

A big thank you and shoutout to my family and my real friends. Thank you, for being by my side through this journey called life. Thank you, for lifting me up over and over again. Thank you for not giving up on me, when I did. Just thank you. I would never have thought I would be writing this book one day. But here I am, also thanks to your support. I know, only I can save myself, but with the right people by my side it's a so much more pleasant journey.